SCIENCE FACTORY
WATER
& BOATS

JON RICHARDS

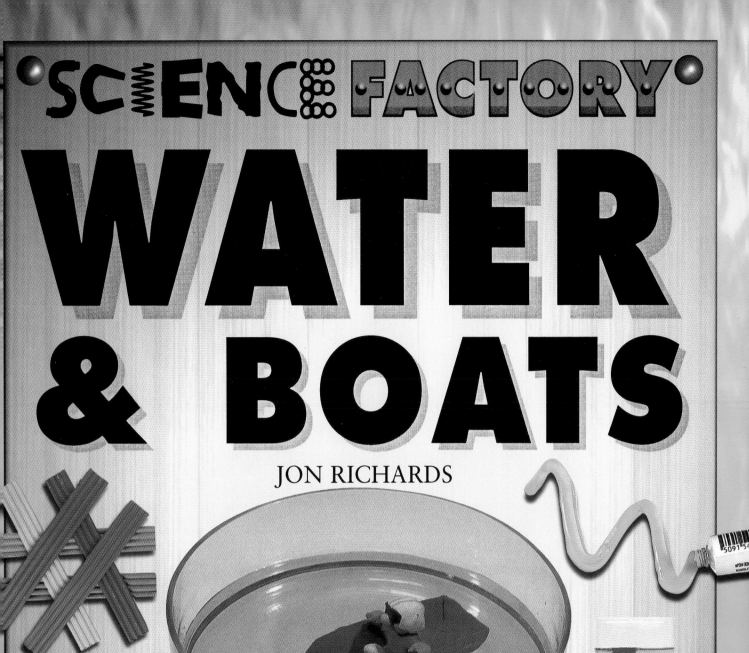

FRANKLIN WATTS
LONDON • SYDNEY

© Aladdin Books Ltd 1999

Designed and produced by
Aladdin Books Ltd
28 Percy Street
London W1P 0LD

ISBN 0 7496 3411 1 (hardback)
ISBN 0 7496 4718 3 (paperback)

First published in Great Britain
in 1999 by
Franklin Watts Books
96 Leonard Street
London EC2A 4RH

Design

David West
Children's Book Design

Designer
Flick Killerby

Illustrator
Ian Moores

Printed in the U.A.E.

A CIP catalogue entry for this book is
available from the British Library.

Some of the illustrations in this series
have appeared in previous books
published by Aladdin Books.

The author, Jon Richards, has written
a number of science and technology
books for children.

Steve Parker, the consultant, has
worked on more than 150 books for
children, mainly on a science theme.

All the photos in this book were
taken by Roger Vlitos.

INTRODUCTION

Water is amazing stuff! It comes
in three different forms – as a
solid, as a liquid and as a gas.
Some objects can float in it,
other objects can sink in it and
a few objects can both float and
sink in it! Water can be used to
turn wheels and it can even
climb dozens of metres against
the force of gravity! Read on
and discover a whole host of
experiments, as well as the
'why-it-works' boxes which will
teach you more about water.

CONTENTS

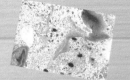

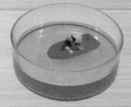

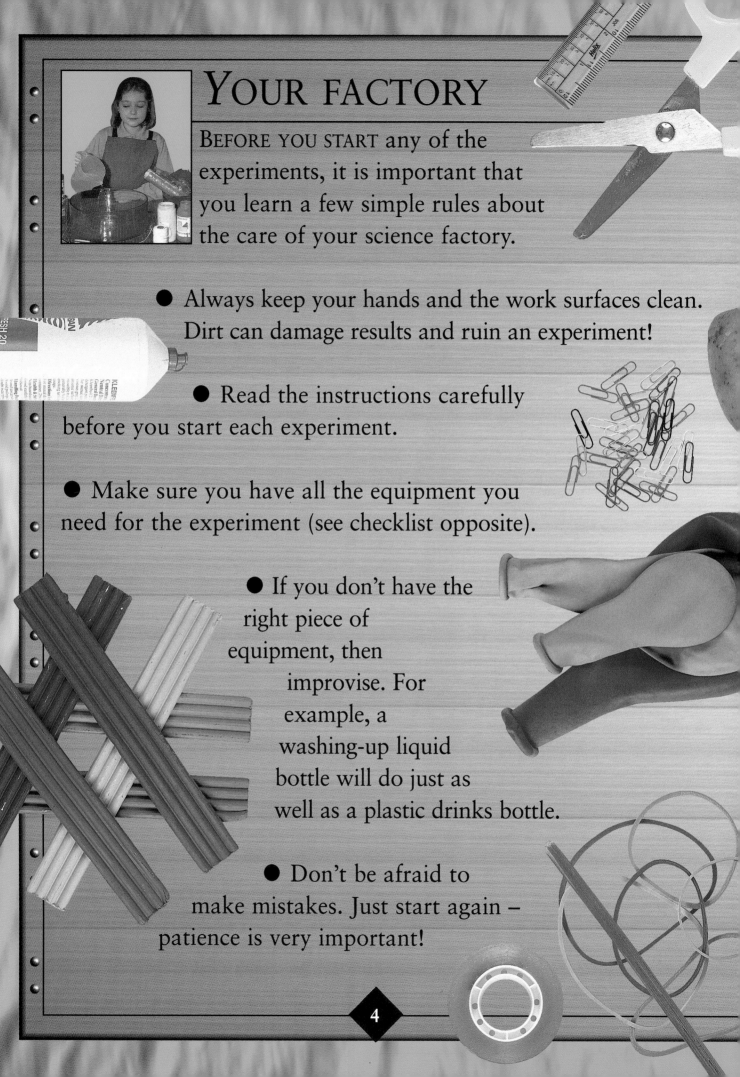

YOUR FACTORY

BEFORE YOU START any of the experiments, it is important that you learn a few simple rules about the care of your science factory.

● Always keep your hands and the work surfaces clean. Dirt can damage results and ruin an experiment!

● Read the instructions carefully before you start each experiment.

● Make sure you have all the equipment you need for the experiment (see checklist opposite).

● If you don't have the right piece of equipment, then improvise. For example, a washing-up liquid bottle will do just as well as a plastic drinks bottle.

● Don't be afraid to make mistakes. Just start again – patience is very important!

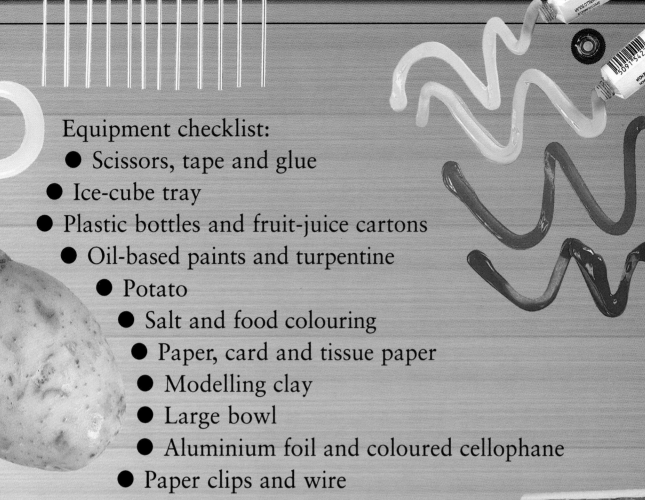

Equipment checklist:
- ● Scissors, tape and glue
- ● Ice-cube tray
- ● Plastic bottles and fruit-juice cartons
- ● Oil-based paints and turpentine
- ● Potato
- ● Salt and food colouring
- ● Paper, card and tissue paper
- ● Modelling clay
- ● Large bowl
- ● Aluminium foil and coloured cellophane
- ● Paper clips and wire
- ● Washing-up liquid
- ● Drinking straws and balloons
- ● Plastic cups and trays
- ● Toothpicks, sticks and matchsticks
- ● Cotton thread
- ● Elastic bands and cling film
- ● Pipe cleaners and bottle caps

WARNING:
Some of the experiments in this book need the help of an adult. Always ask a grown-up to give you a hand when you are using scissors or electrical objects such as hair-dryers!

ICE AND WATER

IF LIQUID WATER IS COOLED ENOUGH, it turns into a solid lump. This solid form of water is called ice. Unlike most substances which shrink when they freeze, water gets larger, or expands, when it turns into ice. Because it expands, it becomes less dense, or lighter than liquid water. This is why ice-cubes float in a drink. This experiment will let you examine the different forms of water, and show you what happens when water freezes and when it melts.

WHAT YOU NEED
Plastic bottle
Food colouring
Ice-cube tray

WHY IT WORKS

As the ice melts, it turns into water. Because this melted ice is cooler than the warm water, it is also more dense. As a result, this freshly melted ice sinks. As it sinks it warms up, becomes less dense, and so rises again.

MELTING ICE-WATER SINKS, IS WARMED, AND SO RISES IN A CIRCULAR CURRENT.

MELTING ICEBERG

1 *Carefully cut the top off a clear plastic drinks bottle. Pour warm water from the tap into the bottle. Add food colouring and stir well.*

2 *Fill another bottle with cold water. Add a few drops of a different food colouring and stir the mixture well. Pour the water into an ice-cube tray and leave it in the freezer overnight.*

6

EXPANDING WATER

This experiment shows that water does expand when it freezes. Fill two plastic bottles with the same amount of water. Place one of them in the freezer overnight. Compare the two bottles the next day. The water placed in the freezer will have frozen and expanded.

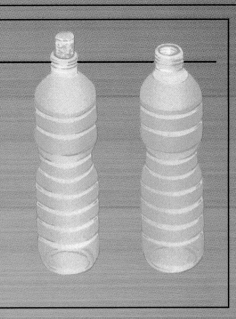

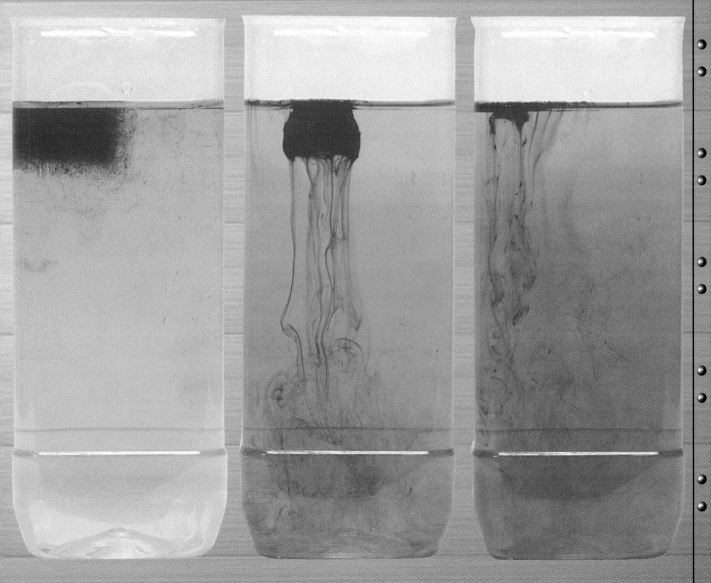

3 Drop one of the coloured ice cubes into the warm water.

4 Watch the melting ice sink to the bottom of the bottle.

SINK AND SWIM

MOST OF THE WATER ON THE EARTH IS IN THE SEAS AND OCEANS. It is called salt water, because it contains salts and minerals that have been washed off the land. Because it contains these salty molecules, salt water is more dense than un-salty water, or fresh water. You can investigate the different densities of salt water and fresh water with this experiment.

WHAT YOU NEED
Potato
Coloured cellophane
Salt
Food colouring
Plastic bottle

FLOATING FISH

1 Cut a thin slice from a potato to make the body of your fish. Cut out a semicircle and a triangular piece from some coloured cellophane – these will form the fins and the tail.

2 Make a slit in the middle of your potato slice and push the cellophane semi-circle through to make the fins above and below the body. Push the cellophane triangle into the back to make the tail.

3 Fill a bottle with cold water and add some salt. Stir this well until all of the salt has disappeared (dissolved). Keep adding salt until no more can dissolve.

4 Fill another bottle with the same amount of water and add some food colouring. Stir this well.

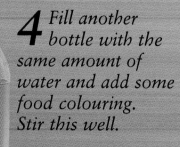

GETTING THE SALT BACK

Ask an adult to boil the salt water in a pan. As the water boils away into steam, the salt is left behind in the pan in a white, crusty layer.

5 *Pour the salty water into a clear plastic bottle from which the top has been cut. Slowly add the coloured water by pouring it over the back of a spoon. Place your fish carefully on the water's surface. Watch the fish sink through the coloured water, but float on top of the salty water.*

WHY IT WORKS

The salt water is more dense than the coloured water, so it will stay at the bottom of the bottle, below the coloured fresh water. Your fish is more dense, or heavier, than the coloured fresh water, but less dense than the salt water. As a result, it will float between the two layers of water.

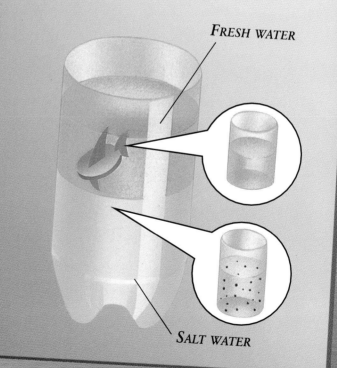

FRESH WATER

SALT WATER

OIL SLICK

WHAT YOU NEED
Oil-based paints
Turpentine
Paper
Large bowl

JUST AS ICE FLOATS IN WATER BECAUSE IT IS LIGHTER, or less dense, so some liquids will float on the surface of water, because they are also less dense. You may have noticed a film of oil floating on top of a puddle on a rainy day. This experiment lets you use floating oil paints to make patterns on paper.

You can make a swirling, multi-coloured pattern with oil-based paints and water.

SWIRLING PATTERNS

1 Mix some different coloured oil-based paints with turpentine to make them thinner.

2 Fill a plastic bowl with cold water and carefully pour small amounts of the paints onto the surface.

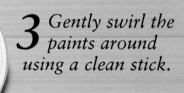

3 Gently swirl the paints around using a clean stick.

4 Carefully lower a sheet of paper on top of the paint. Allow the paper to soak up some of the paint, then peel off the paper and see what patterns have been left on it by the paint.

WHY IT WORKS

The paint floats on the surface of the water because it is less dense than the water. As a result, you can pick up the colours by placing your paper on top.

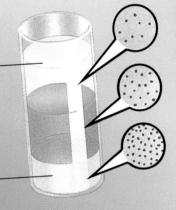

OIL FLOATS ON TOP OF WATER BECAUSE IT IS LESS DENSE.

SALT WATER SITS BENEATH FRESH WATER BECAUSE IT IS MORE DENSE.

FLOATING STRAWS

A hydrometer is a device which measures density. You can make one using a drinking straw and some modelling clay. The hydrometer will float higher in dense liquids than in less-dense liquids.

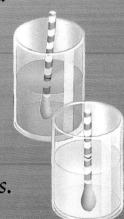

SHIPSHAPE

ENORMOUS AIRCRAFT CARRIERS AND LARGE CRUISE SHIPS float, yet a single metal screw will sink! When it comes to floating, size is not important. Instead, whether something floats or not depends on the weight of the water displaced by the object when it sits in the water. If this displaced water weighs more than the object, then the object will float.

CRAFTY VESSELS

1 *Mould a lump of modelling clay into different solid shapes and see if they will float in a bowl of water.*

2 *Now roll the clay flat. Curve the edges up and pinch them together to form a boat shape. Make sure your boat doesn't leak!*

3 *Gently place your boat into the bowl of water and see if it floats. Mark on the side of your boat the level to which the water reaches.*

4 *Now make a clay figure to sit in the middle of your boat. Put the boat back in the water and you will see that the boat now sits lower in the water than when it was empty.*

WHY IT WORKS

When you make your boat shape, the volume of water displaced by the boat weighs more than the boat, so it floats. When you add your clay passenger, you are increasing the weight of the boat, so it sinks slightly into the water.

FLOAT OR SINK?

Try making different shapes of boat. A high-sided boat will float better than a shallow one. This is because it can sit lower in the water without having water spill over its sides. Now try some other boat shapes and see which will carry the heaviest load.

HIGH-SIDED BOAT

WATER FLOWS OVER SIDES OF BOAT

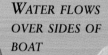

LOW-SIDED BOAT

REACHING THE DEPTHS

Unlike boats, submarines can sink and float as many times as they want. They do this by pumping air or water into special tanks inside them. If a submarine pumps water into these tanks, then it becomes heavier and sinks. If it pumps air into these tanks, then the submarine becomes lighter and rises towards the surface. Build your own submersible and see how it can sink and float as many times as you like!

Squeeze the sides of the bottle and watch your submersible dive to the bottom. Release the bottle and your submersible will rise to the top.

BOTTLED SUBMERSIBLE

1 To make your submersible, cut the ribbed part off a flexible drinking straw and bend it in half.

2 Open up a metal paper clip and push each end into each end of the bent straw. Make sure that the paper clip will not slide out.

3 Roll out three thin strips of modelling clay. Loop and pinch each one around the paper clip. These strips will weigh your submersible down.

4 Place your submersible in a glass of water to test that it floats the right way up. Alter the amount of modelling clay until it just floats.

WHY IT WORKS

Trapped inside the straw is a bubble of air. When you squeeze the bottle, water is pushed into the straw and squashes the air bubble. As a result, your submersible becomes heavier and sinks.

5 Place your submersible in a large plastic bottle full of water. Screw on the top securely.

UNDER PRESSURE

Stretch cling film over the top of a tub of water and secure it with an elastic band. Push on the cling film – does your submersible still sink?

CLIMBING WATER

HAVE YOU EVER WONDERED how plants can get water to every branch, stem and leaf? This is due to a process called capillary action. It involves very long and very thin tubes which lie inside the plant. Forces inside these very narrow tubes actually draw water up. In the tallest trees, water can be pulled up dozens of metres!

WHAT YOU NEED
Thin card
Large bowl
Glue

CHANGING COLOUR

Put some coloured water in a vase of water with a flower. Over a couple of days the flower will draw the coloured water up its stem and its flower will change colour.

PAPER PETALS

1 Take a square piece of smooth writing paper or thin card and fold it in half. Do not use shiny paper.

2 Now fold the paper in half again to form a square.

3 Fold it in half again, this time to form a triangle.

4 Cut the shape of a petal out of the side with the thickest fold. Unfold the paper and you will have your flower.

7 Place your flowers in a bowl of water. Watch as the petals of your flowers unfurl as the water seeps into the paper.

5 Using a pencil or a straw, roll the petals of the flower so that the petals remain closed.

6 Brighten up your flower by sticking a circle of different coloured paper in the centre. Make some other flowers of different shapes and colours.

WHY IT WORKS

Like the stem of a plant, the paper is full of tiny tubes called capillaries. An attractive force between the molecules of water and the sides of these tiny tubes is strong enough to draw water up. As the water rises, the paper becomes heavy and the petals unfurl.

WATER LEVEL

CAPILLARY TUBES IN PAPER

WALKING ON WATER

IF YOU SPILL SOME WATER ONTO A FLAT SURFACE you will see that the drops of water will clump together – almost as if they are held together by an invisible skin. You can also see this if you fill a tall glass with water right to the very top. The water will appear to bulge ever so slightly above the top of the glass. Some insects use this invisible skin and can actually walk on water!

WHAT YOU NEED
Paper clips
Aluminium foil
Tissue paper
Washing-up liquid

WATER WALKERS

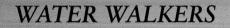

1 Use some paper clips and wide strips of foil to make your water walkers.

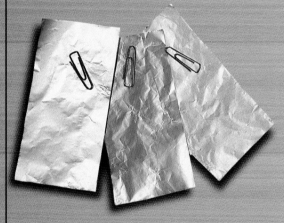

2 Wrap each paper clip in a strip of foil and twist three legs out of the foil on either side of your water walker. Colour your water walkers with bright colours.

3 Place your water walkers on a sheet of tissue paper. Hold the tissue tightly and gently lower it onto the surface of a bowl of water.

4 The tissue will gradually soak up the water and sink to the bottom, but your water walkers will rest on the surface.

WHY IT WORKS

Water molecules are attracted to each other. On the surface, this attraction pulls the molecules together, producing a force called surface tension. This force is strong enough to support some light objects.

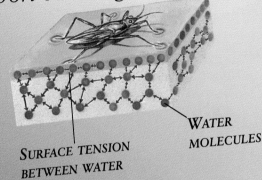

SURFACE TENSION BETWEEN WATER MOLECULES

WATER MOLECULES

MOVING INSECTS

Washing-up liquid breaks up the water's surface tension. By dropping some liquid between your water walkers, you will make them dart away from each other.

THE POWER OF WATER

UNLIKE AIR, LIQUIDS CANNOT BE SQUASHED. This makes liquids very useful in lifting heavy objects, from raising the bed of a tipper truck to stretching the arm of a large digger. This use of liquids to lift and move objects is called hydraulics. Build your own hydraulic machine which will show you how water can be used to lift loads.

LIQUID LIFT

1 Carefully cut the tops off two plastic bottles and make them the same height.

2 Pierce a hole in the side of each bottle a short distance up from the bottom. Push a drinking straw through the holes to link the bottles. Use modelling clay to seal the joins and make them watertight.

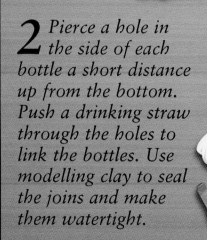

3 A plastic cup and a lump of modelling clay will act as a load, while a balloon will help you apply pressure.

4 Colour some water with food colouring and fill the bottles so that they are about two-thirds full. Float the cup in one bottle and place the lump of modelling clay in the cup.

20

WHY IT WORKS

When you push down on the balloon, it forces water through the straw, transferring the force of your push into the other bottle. More water now sits in the other bottle, so the cup sits higher than it used to.

DOWNWARD FORCE

LOAD IS RAISED

UPWARD FORCE

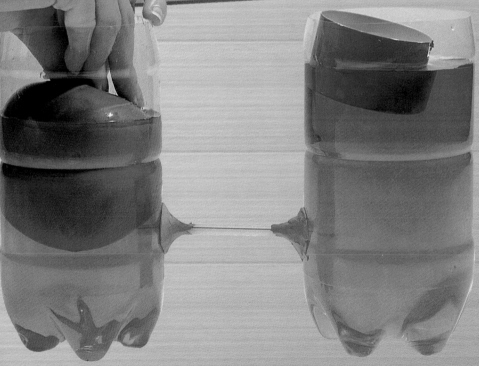

5 Inflate the balloon a little and place it in the other bottle. The balloon must press and slide against the bottle's sides. Now push down on the balloon and watch the cup and the modelling clay rise in the other bottle.

CHANGING THE SYSTEM

Try using bottles of different sizes. You will find that a tall, narrow bottle will raise the load the highest because the displaced water has to fit into a narrower bottle.

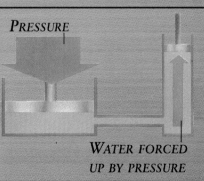

PRESSURE

WATER FORCED UP BY PRESSURE

WATER JETS

BECAUSE OF GRAVITY, WATER USUALLY FLOWS DOWNHILL – however, it
can be made to shoot up into the air! These jets of water can be
natural, such as geysers, or artificial, such as fountains.
This experiment lets you build
your own fountain. See how high
you can make your jet of water
soar up into the air.

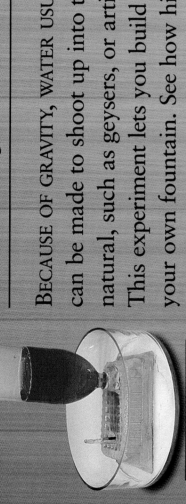

LIQUID JETS

1 Carefully cut
the bottom off
a large plastic
drinks bottle.

WHY IT WORKS

*The fountain is caused by the weight
of the water in the upturned bottle.
This weight causes a build-up of
pressure. The more water there is in
the bottle, the greater the
pressure and the higher
your fountain will soar.
This pressure is released
when the water
squirts out of the
U-shaped bend.*

WATER IN BOTTLE
CAUSES PRESSURE

PRESSURE OF WATER
CAUSES FOUNTAIN

2 Seal the mouth of the bottle with some modelling clay and poke a straw through into the bottle. Fit another straw to the end of the first straw to form a U-shaped bend.

3 Pierce two holes in the bottom of a plastic tray. Turn the bottle upside down and feed the straw tube through the holes. Seal the bottle in position over one of the holes using modelling clay.

4 Place the tray in a shallow tub. Fill the upturned bottle and watch a fountain spurt from the other end of the U-shaped drinking-straw tube.

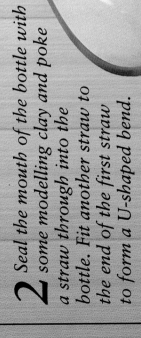

A FALL IN PRESSURE

Pierce holes down the side of a plastic bottle. Fill the bottle with water and watch how far the jets of water squirt. The jets at the bottom, where the pressure is greatest, will squirt farther than those at the top.

WATERWORKS

WATER HAS BEEN USED as a source of power for thousands of years. Since Roman times, wooden water-wheels have powered millstones to grind corn into flour. Today, enormous dams channel fast-flowing water past the modern version of the wooden water-wheel – the turbine. This spins to make electricity.

WHAT YOU NEED
Plastic bottles
Drinking straw
Tape
Toothpicks
Matchstick
Stick
Cotton thread
Large bowl
Bottle cap

Place the water-wheel in a bowl. Pour water into the upside-down bottle. Watch as water pours onto your water-wheel, causing it to spin and raise the bucket.

WHY IT WORKS

The water-wheel uses the energy of the falling water to make it spin. As it spins, the wheel winds up the thread, raising the bucket.

FALLING WATER SPINS THE WHEEL

WATER POWER

1 Cut the bottom off a washing-up liquid bottle to make your water-wheel. Cut out four flaps from the side of the wheel. Bend these flaps as shown to make the wheel's blades. Make a hole in the centre of the wheel.

2 Cut a section out of the bottom of a plastic drinks bottle, large enough for the wheel to fit into. Pierce holes on either side of this section.

3 Fit the water-wheel into the cut-out section by passing a drinking straw through the holes in the bottle and the hole in the wheel. Attach the wheel to the straw using modelling clay. Poke toothpicks through the ends of the straw to hold it in place.

4 Pierce holes in the top of the drinks bottle and feed a stick through. Tape a length of drinking straw to one end of the stick.

5 Make a bucket using a bottle cap. Glue a matchstick across the the top of the cap and tie a length of cotton thread to the matchstick. Feed the cotton through the short length of straw and tie it around a toothpick pushed through the straw holding the water-wheel.

6 Fix another upside-down bottle on top, having cut off its bottom and sealed its top, leaving only a small hole.

GETTING HEAVY

Try adding small modelling-clay weights to the bucket. See how this affects the speed at which the bucket is lifted. You will find that with more weight to lift, the wheel will find it harder to raise the bucket. You could also try raising the height of the upside-down bottle – how does this affect the wheel?

PADDLING AWAY

WHAT YOU NEED

*Small plastic
drinks bottle
Card
Two sticks
Fruit-juice
carton
Modelling clay
Elastic band*

SOME OF THE EARLIEST POWERED BOATS WERE CALLED PADDLE-STEAMERS. They used wheels, either at the rear of the boat or hung on its sides, to push the vessel through the water. However, the age of the paddle steamer was short-lived. Before long, boat builders found that propellers were better at pushing boats. Paddle-steamers can still be seen today, but mostly as tourist attractions.

PADDLE POWER

1 *Screw the top of a small plastic drinks bottle on tightly. Cut a hole in the side of the bottle where the boat's funnel will sit.*

2 *Tape two sticks to the sides of the bottle so that they stick out past the bottle's bottom.*

3 *Cut two rectangles from a fruit-juice carton, making sure that they are not as wide as the plastic drinks bottle.*

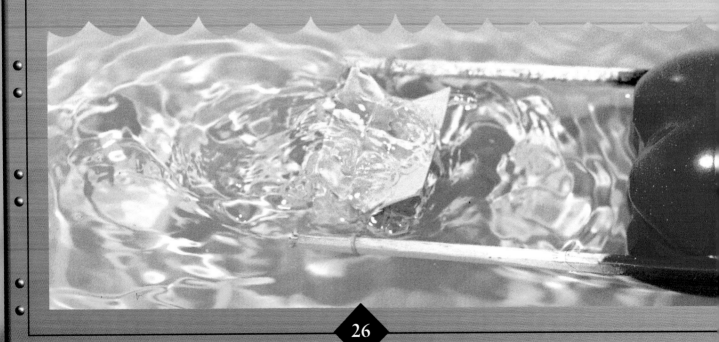

4 Make a slit halfway down each rectangle and slide the two together to form a cross-shaped paddle.

5 Tape an elastic band to the paddle and fix the ends of the band around the sticks. Make sure that the paddle does not touch the boat.

6 Weigh down the boat by placing a lump of modelling clay in the bottle. Cover the hole in the bottle with a cardboard funnel. Wind up the elastic band and place your boat in a bath of water. Watch as the paddle spins and the boat moves forward.

WHY IT WORKS

When you wind the elastic band, you are storing energy in it. This energy is released when you let go of the paddle, causing it to spin. As it spins, the blades push against the water, moving the boat forward.

BOAT'S MOVEMENT

SPINNING PADDLE WHEEL

SIZE MATTERS

Try different sizes of paddle wheel on your boat. You will find that a larger wheel will push the boat along more quickly than a small one.

27

STEERING

FISH USE FINS ON THEIR BODIES TO STEER THEMSELVES THROUGH THE WATER. Similarly, boats have one fin at the rear which is used to steer – it's called a rudder. As well as a rudder, submarines have fins on their bodies, just like fish. They can use these fins to move the submarine up and down as well as from side to side as it travels underwater.

WHAT YOU
NEED
Wire
Drinking straw
Fruit-juice
carton
Paddle-boat
made on pages
26-27

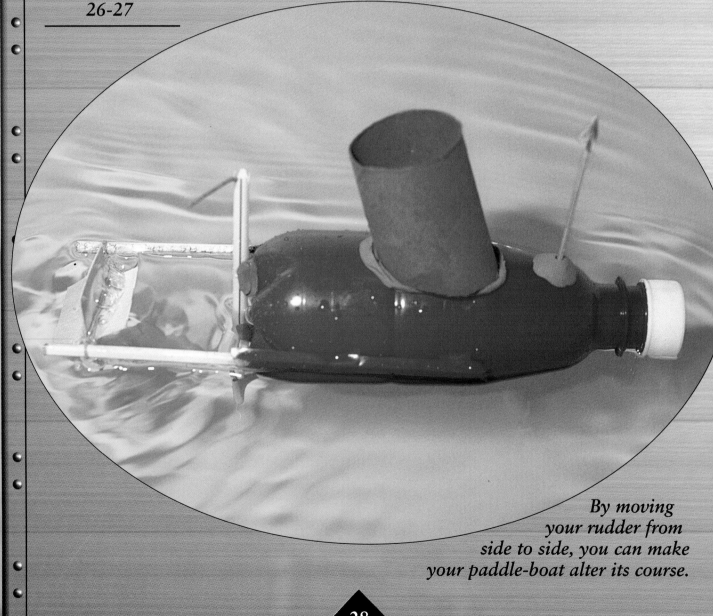

By moving your rudder from side to side, you can make your paddle-boat alter its course.

WHY IT WORKS

The rudder works by deflecting the water, causing the boat to alter its course. If the rudder points straight back, then the boat will go straight on (1). If the rudder is turned to the right, then the boat will steer right (2) and left if the rudder is turned to the left (3).

SUBMARINE STEERING

Make a submarine out of a lump of modelling clay. Fix four fins to the sides, two at the front and two at the back. Adjust these fins to point up or down. See how they affect your submarine's descent through a bottle of water.

SUBMARINE WITH FINS

RUDDER CONTROL

1 To make a rudder, bend a piece of wire to form a right angle, making the handle of your rudder.

2 Cut out a small square from a fruit juice carton. Slide the wire through a length of straw and fix the square to the bottom of the wire. Fix the straw to the back of the paddle-boat made on pages 26-27.

3 Wind up the paddle and place the boat in a bath of water. As the boat moves forward, turn the handle of the rudder from one side to the other, and see what this does to your boat's course.

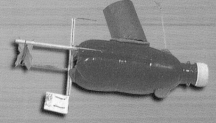

FINDING OUT MORE

BOILING The process of turning a liquid into a gas by raising its temperature. You can boil liquid water to turn it into steam.

CAPILLARY ACTION The movement of a liquid along very narrow tubes.

DENSITY The heaviness of a substance for a particular volume.

FREEZING The process of turning a liquid into a solid by lowering its temperature.

FRESH WATER Water which has very few dissolved substances, such as salts and minerals.

GRAVITY The attractive force between objects. The Earth's gravity keeps us on the ground.

FLOATING CITY

The largest aircraft carriers need nearly 6,500 people to run them!

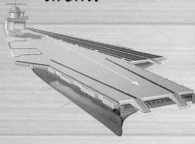

HYDRAULICS The technology of liquids

HYDROMETER An instrument used to compare the densities of different liquids.

ICE The solid form of water. Water freezes and turns into ice when the temperature gets below 0°C.

FAST BOAT

The fastest boat in the world is called Spirit of Australia. *It reached an incredible speed of 522 km/h (276 knots)!*

HYDROFOILS

Some boats have wings! Hydrofoils use their wings to lift them out of the water, allowing them to move more easily.

MELTING the process of turning a solid into a liquid by raising its temperature.

MOLECULE The smallest naturally occurring particle of a substance.

RUDDER A special paddle usually found at the rear of a boat. It is used to steer the boat.

SALT WATER Water which contains a high level of salts and minerals. These give the water a salty taste.

STEAM The gas form of water. Water boils and turns into steam when it is heated to 100°C.

EARLY SUB

The Turtle *was the first submarine to be used in battle. In 1776 it was used to try and sink a British warship.*

SUBMERSIBLE A craft which can go underwater and rise again to the surface at will.

SURFACE TENSION The attractive force between molecules at the surface of a liquid.

WATER-WHEEL

A wheel which is turned by flowing water. Today, water-wheels, or turbines, are used to produce electricity.

INDEX